W9-ALU-400

Ripley's
Believe It or Not!®

WEIRD INVENTIONS AND DISCOVERIES

A Byron Preiss Book

TOR

A TOM DOHERTY ASSOCIATES BOOK
NEW YORK

Ripley's Believe It or Not!
Weird Inventions and Discoveries

Copyright © 1990 by Ripley's Entertainment, Inc.
Cover design copyright © 1990 by Byron Preiss Visual Publications, Inc.
Cover design by Dean Motter
Edited by Howard Zimmerman

Special thanks to the following people for their help in
producing this book: Mary Higgins, William Mohalley, Stephen
Brenninkmeyer, Kim Kindya, and Kathleen Doherty

A TOR Book
Published by Tom Doherty Associates, Inc.
49 West 24th Street
New York, NY 10010

ISBN: 0-812-51284-7

First Tor edition: May 1991

Printed in the United States of America

0 9 8 7 6 5 4 3 2 1

INTRODUCTION

Welcome to the special Centennial Edition of "Ripley's Believe It or Not!", the most famous and best known entertainment feature in the world. The centennial series is designed to help celebrate the forthcoming hundredth anniversary of Robert L. Ripley's birth in 1993.

Ripley was one of the most fabulous and interesting personalities of the 20th century. He spent his life traveling the globe in pursuit of the odd, bizarre, and incredible-but-true stories that have filled the "Believe It or Not!" pages for over 70 years. During this period, more than 80 million people in 125 countries have been entertained and amazed by Robert L. Ripley's creation. In addition, millions more have marveled at the incredible oddities on display at the Ripley's museums in America, Canada, and Australia.

Ripley's amazing worldwide industry is a true American success story, for it started humbly with one man and an idea.

In 1918, the twenty-five-year-old Ripley was a hard-working sports cartoonist for the New York Globe newspaper. It happened one day that he was stuck for a cartoon to draw. As his daily deadline approached, he was still staring at a blank sheet on his drawing board when inspiration struck. Ripley dug into his files where he kept notes on all sorts of unusual sports achievements. He quickly sketched nine of the more interesting and bizarre items onto his page, and a legend was born. That first page was titled "Champs and Chumps." Ripley's editor quickly came up with a snappier name, and "Believe It or Not!" became an overnight sensation.

In 1929, Ripley published his very first collection of "Believe It or Not!" in book form. It was an immediate success. A few years later his feature was appearing in over 200 newspapers in the United States and Canada alone. But Ripley was just getting started. With financial backing from his newspaper syndicate, Ripley traveled thousands of miles in the next few years. He visited 198 countries, bringing back oddities, antiques, and amazing stories from each place he stopped. The best of these eventually wound up in his famous syndicated feature. The amazing truth is that Ripley supplied at least one "Believe It or Not!" every day for thirty years!

In 1933, Ripley collected many of his fabulous treasures and put them on exhibition in Chicago. Within a year, his "Odditorium" had hosted almost two and a half million people. They lined up around the block to see the displays of shrunken heads, postage-stamp-size paintings, treasures from the Orient, incredibly intricate matchstick models, and wickedly gleaming instruments of medieval torture.

Soon after Ripley died in 1949, his unique collection of oddities was gathered and displayed in the first permanent "Believe It or Not!" museum in St. Augustine, Florida. And, fittingly, Ripley himself became one of its more amazing items. A full-size replica of the man stood at the door, greeting all visitors and giving them a foretaste of the astonishing objects they would see inside.

Although Robert L. Ripley passed away, his work lives on. The Ripley's organization has ceaselessly provided daily "Believe It or Not!" pages through the decades, always reaching a bit farther for those fantastic (but true) stories that stretch the imagination. And they are still actively seeking more. If you know of any amazing oddity, write it down and send it in to:

Ripley's Believe It or Not!
90 Eglinton Avenue East, Suite 510
Toronto, Canada
M4P 2Y3

There are now over 110,000 "Believe It or Not!" cartoons that have been printed in over 300 categories. This includes everything from amazing animals to catastrophes to "Weird Inventions and Discoveries," the volume you hold right now. So sit back, get comfortable, and prepare to be astonished, surprised, amazed and delighted. Believe it or not!

PINK LEMONADE

WAS CREATED IN 1857 BY PETE CONKLIN WHO UN-WITTINGLY USED A BUCKET OF WATER IN WHICH A CIRCUS PER-FORMER HAD SOAKED HIS RED TIGHTS

THE PRE-HISTORIC HORSE THAT EXISTS UNCHANGED TODAY

PRZEWALSKI'S HORSE DISCOVERED IN 1881 BY THE EXPLORER, COLONEL N.M. PRZEVALSKI, AND FOUND IN A WILD STATE ONLY ON THE MONGOLIAN STEPPES, IS *EXACTLY AS IT WAS IN THE ICE AGE*

THE REAL McCOY

ELIJAH McCOY (1843-1929)
INVENTED A LUBRICATION SYSTEM SO
POPULAR THAT BUSINESSMEN INSPECTING
NEW EQUIPMENT ROUTINELY INQUIRED
IF IT HAD "THE REAL McCOY"

THE SPACE JUNKMAN
EDUARDO CARRION SAN JUAN of San José, Calif., INVENTED AND DESIGNED THE LUNAR VEHICLE USED TO EXPLORE THE MOON --- HIS PROTOTYPE WAS BUILT *FROM SCRAP ALUMINUM, AN OLD UMBRELLA, BICYCLE HANDLEBARS, AUTOMOBILE HUBCAPS, STARTER MOTOR, BATTERIES AND ARMY SURPLUS STOCK!*

A TOPCOAT PATENTED BY HOWARD ROSS OF GAINESVILLE, VA., IN 1953, COULD BE WORN BY ONE PERSON -- OR SERVED AS A DOUBLE COAT FOR TWO PEOPLE

SIR THOMAS URQUHART,
A 17TH CENTURY ENGLISH
TRANSLATOR, INVENTED A
LANGUAGE IN WHICH *ALL
THE WORDS COULD BE
READ FORWARD OR
BACKWARD !*

AN **8-MAN TRICYCLE** BUILT IN NEW ENGLAND IN 1896 WEIGHED **2,500** POUNDS, WAS **17** FEET IN LENGTH, AND *ITS REAR WHEELS WERE 11 FEET IN DIAMETER*

A **RAILROAD SYSTEM**

FEATURING CARS WITH TRACKS ON SLOPED ROOFS WAS PATENTED BY HENRY LATIMER SIMMONS, OF WICKES, MONTANA, IN 1895, *--SO ONE TRAIN COULD LEAPFROG OVER ANOTHER ON A SINGLE TRACK*

IN 1940, GEORGE DE MAESTRAL, A SWISS SCIENTIST, INVENTED VELCRO AFTER STUDYING BURS HE FOUND CLINGING TO HIS TROUSERS WHILE WALKING IN THE WOODS!

DR. GIDEON ALGERNON MANTELL (1790-1852) A PHYSICIAN AT CUCKFIELD, SUSSEX, ENGLAND, *WAS THE FIRST MAN TO FIND AND DESCRIBE A DINOSAUR*

THOMAS EDISON (1847-1931) THE 20TH CENTURY'S GREATEST INVENTOR, WAS DEEPLY INTERESTED IN THE PSYCHIC WORLD AND WAS FOOLED BY A CHARLATAN USING **LIGHTS, A PHONOGRAPH AND OTHER EDISON CREATIONS** TO SEND AND RECEIVE "PSYCHIC MESSAGES"-- *EDISON, HIMSELF, INVENTED, BUT NEVER PATENTED, A MACHINE FOR "COMMUNICATING" WITH THE DEAD.*

A **MUSTACHE PROTECTOR** DEVISED BY ELI J. F. RANDOLPH, OF N.Y., IN 1872, WAS A HARD-RUBBER DEVICE WITH PRONGS THAT FITTED INTO THE NOSTRILS TO KEEP *THE MUSTACHE DRY WHEN EATING AND DRINKING*

THE LUNAR SOCIETY

of Birmingham, England, formed in the 1760s comprised a group of philosophers and inventors who adopted that name because they met on the Monday night nearest to the full moon so it would light their way home — but the distinguished members eventually came to be known as *"THE LUNATICS"*

THE FIRST PRESS USING MOVABLE TYPE, INVENTED BY JOHANNES GUTENBERG IN 1440, WAS ADAPTED FROM THE MACHINES USED TO *PRESS GRAPES AND CHEESE*

EYEGLASSES
seen by Marco Polo
in China in 1275 A.D.
— were actually
invented by the
Chinese as early
as 500 B.C.

THE FIRST U.S. ARMY AIRCRAFT
WAS A DIRIGIBLE PURCHASED IN 1908, BUT IT WAS NEVER
USED BECAUSE T.S. BALDWIN, ITS INVENTOR, **WAS THE
ONLY ONE WHO COULD FLY IT**

THE
WORLD'S
BIGGEST
COMPUTER
PRINTER

MANUFACTURED IN JAPAN, IS NEARLY 70 FEET LONG, 9 FEET IN
HEIGHT AND WEIGHS 14 TONS... ALTHOUGH IT TAKES AN HOUR
AND ONE HALF, IT CAN PRINT AN ENTIRE 4-COLOR BILLBOARD
50-FEET WIDE IN ONE MOTION

ALFRED B.
NOBEL
INVENTOR
OF DYNAMITE
WHICH CAUSED THE DEATH OF MILLIONS OF
SOLDIERS IN WARS ALL OVER THE WORLD!

IS THE DONOR OF THE GREATEST
AWARD FOR PEACE ——
THE NOBEL PEACE PRIZE

SAMUEL COLT (1814-1862) INVENTOR OF THE REVOLVER THAT BEARS HIS NAME, *GOT THE IDEA FOR ITS REVOLVING CYLINDER* AS A 16-YEAR-OLD SEAMAN WATCHING THE HELMSMAN TURN THE SHIP'S WHEEL--EACH SPOKE ALIGNING WITH A CLUTCH THAT HELD IT FAST

CHESTER GREENWOOD (1858-1937) INVENTED EARMUFFS AT THE AGE OF 15

IN 1760, JOSEPH MERLIN, A BELGIAN MUSICIAN, INVENTED ROLLER SKATES AND DEMONSTRATED THEM AT A BALL BY SKATING ACROSS THE ROOM WHILE PLAYING THE VIOLIN!

"GILLS" FOR HUMANS

THE HEMOSPONGE, AN EXPERIMENTAL DEVICE BEING DEVELOPED WITH SUPPORT FROM THE U.S. OFFICE OF NAVAL RESEARCH, MAY MAKE IT POSSIBLE FOR DIVERS TO REMAIN SUBMERGED FOR SEVERAL DAYS, *EXTRACTING OXYGEN FROM THE WATER*

A COMPUTERIZED ROBOT "GUIDE DOG"

DESIGNED IN JAPAN, EMITS ULTRA-SOUND WAVES THAT BOUNCE OFF OBSTACLES TO GUIDE A BLIND PERSON AROUND THEM OR, IF IT IS NOT SAFE TO PROCEED, IT WAITS UNTIL THE OBSTACLE DISAPPEARS AND CAN EVEN **PLOT THE BEST ROUTE FROM START TO FINISH !**

WIND
DIRECTION INDICATOR
INVENTED BY
THOMAS JEFFERSON
HE COULD TELL WHICH WAY
THE WIND BLEW WITHOUT
GOING OUT OF DOORS.

Indicator was Attached
to the Ceiling

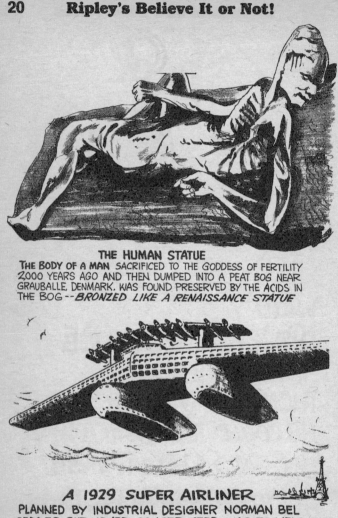

THE HUMAN STATUE

THE BODY OF A MAN SACRIFICED TO THE GODDESS OF FERTILITY 2,000 YEARS AGO AND THEN DUMPED INTO A PEAT BOG NEAR GRAUBALLE, DENMARK, WAS FOUND PRESERVED BY THE ACIDS IN THE BOG -- *BRONZED LIKE A RENAISSANCE STATUE*

A 1929 SUPER AIRLINER

PLANNED BY INDUSTRIAL DESIGNER NORMAN BEL GEDDES, BUT NEVER CONSTRUCTED, WAS TO WEIGH 700 TONS, HAVE 20 ENGINES, ACCOMMODATIONS FOR 451 PASSENGERS AND A CREW OF 155, FLY AT 90 MPH AND CROSS THE ATLANTIC 3 TIMES A WEEK! ITS COST OF $9,000,000 WAS PROHIBITIVE TO INVESTORS

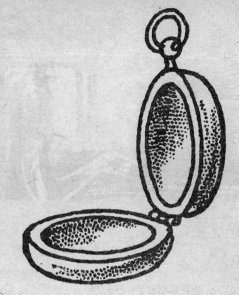

PARKING SPACE
FOR GUM
INVENTED BY
C.W. ROBERTSON
SOMERVILLE, Tenn.
PATENT NO.
395,515

A STREET CAR

INVENTED BY I.M.S.R. MATHEWSON
of Gilroy, Calif., in 1876
HAD ITS GASOLINE MOTOR
DISGUISED AS THE HEAD
OF A HORSE

*-SO IT WOULD
NOT FRIGHTEN
REAL HORSES*

BIOLOGISTS

HAVE IDENTIFIED AND STUDIED
LESS THAN 10% OF THE PLANT
AND ANIMAL SPECIES ON
EARTH... MILLIONS MORE MAY
DISAPPEAR BEFORE THEY
ARE EVEN DISCOVERED.

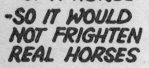

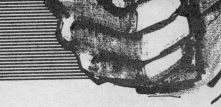

A GUN

INVENTED BY RUDY ORTEGA AND MIKE ASKEW OF JACKSONVILLE, FLA., HAS A CAMERA IN ITS BUTT WHICH TAKES A PICTURE 0.25 SECONDS BEFORE IT IS FIRED -- GIVING CONCLUSIVE EVIDENCE WHETHER OR NOT THE PERSON FIRED AT *WAS ARMED*

SHOOTING CURVES!

A MECHANICAL BASEBALL PITCHER
WAS INVENTED BY PROF. C.H. MINTONI, Princeton, N.J.

THE CURVING OF THE BALL
WAS ACCOMPLISHED BY
2 STEEL FINGERS
PROJECTING FROM
THE MOUTH OF THE GUN

PATENT
#748,284

A METHOD
FOR *PRESERVING A DEAD
BODY IN A SEALED TRANS-
PARENT BLOCK OF GLASS*
WAS REGISTERED AT THE U.S.
PATENT OFFICE IN 1903!

SCREAM MUFFLER

A NEW INVENTION ENABLES STRESS-RIDDEN PEOPLE TO RELIEVE THEIR TENSIONS BY SCREAMING INTO A SMALL SPHERE PACKED WITH ACOUSTICAL FOAM THAT MAKES THE LOUDEST SCREAM SOUND LIKE POLITE CONVERSATION

PATENT # 889,928

A PATENT FOR AN ALARM CLOCK THAT *SPRAYS WATER ON THE FACE OF A SLEEPING PERSON* WAS FILED AT THE U.S. PATENT OFFICE IN 1907!

THE **NEW WORLD** WAS FOUNDED ON *Christmas Eve!*
THE SANTA MARIA, FLAGSHIP OF CHRISTOPHER COLUMBUS, WAS WRECKED OFF CAP-HAITIEN, HAITI, ON DECEMBER 24th, 1492, AND HIS MEN SET TO WORK IMMEDIATELY TO BUILD A FORT -- WHICH BECAME *THE FIRST PERMANENT SETTLEMENT IN AMERICA !*

A **MECHANICAL ALTAR** OPERATED BY STEAM, INVENTED BY AN EGYPTIAN NAMED HERON, OF ALEXANDRIA, 1,900 YEARS AGO--

2 MECHANICAL FIGURES POURED FROM JARS A LIQUID WHICH STARTED A FIRE ON THE ALTAR, CAUSING A MECHANICAL SERPENT TO WRIGGLE AND HISS AROUND A SACRIFICIAL VASE

ALEXANDER GRAHAM BELL (1847-1922) INVENTOR OF THE TELEPHONE, REFUSED TO KEEP ONE IN HIS STUDY BECAUSE THE *RINGING DISTRACTED HIM FROM HIS THOUGHTS*

THE **MAN** WHOSE NAME IS
WRITTEN IN THE STARS
GEORG FISCHBERG (1789-1873)
A BOOKKEEPER AT THE IMPERIAL
ASTRONOMICAL OBSERVATORY, IN VIENNA,
AUSTRIA, ON HIS OWN TIME AT NIGHT
DISCOVERED 81 NEW STARS
—ALL OF WHICH BEAR HIS NAME

A **GUN**
INVENTED IN
GERMANY
DURING
WORLD WAR II
*ACTUALLY COULD
SHOOT AROUND
A CORNER*

NEW ANIMAL SPECIES
12,100 WERE DISCOVERED EVERY
YEAR BETWEEN 1900 AND 1950 ···
SINCE THEN 5,200 HAVE BEEN
FOUND ANNUALLY ··· SCIENTISTS
ESTIMATE THERE ARE 30,000,000
UNDISCOVERED SPECIES··· OVER 70% OF
ALL KNOWN SPECIES ARE INSECTS···

JOHN DEE (1527-1608)
famed English mathematician and Warden
of Manchester College
WAS THE INVENTOR OF THE
FORTUNE TELLER'S CRYSTAL BALL
1580

A **LOCOMOTIVE** OPERATED BY COMPRESSED AIR WAS INVENTED BY ANDRAUD, A FRENCHMAN, IN 1840 *BECAUSE HE FEARED THE WORLD WAS RUNNING OUT OF COAL*

A "DEATH RAY" PISTOL
DEMONSTRATED IN PARIS, FRANCE, IN 1934 FIRED MAGNESIUM CHARGES AND WAS CLAIMED TO BE CAPABLE OF STUNNING MEN AND ANIMALS *AT A DISTANCE OF ONE MILE*

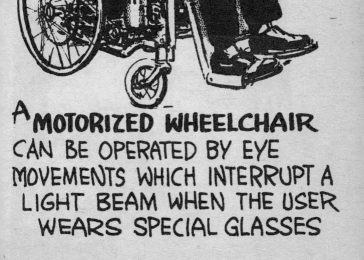

A **MOTORIZED WHEELCHAIR**
CAN BE OPERATED BY EYE
MOVEMENTS WHICH INTERRUPT A
LIGHT BEAM WHEN THE USER
WEARS SPECIAL GLASSES

SE-QUO-YAH
(Cherokee)
AN INDIAN WHO COULD NEITHER READ
NOR WRITE INVENTED THE ONLY
WRITTEN ALPHABET USED BY THE
NORTH AMERICAN INDIANS

THE
SAFETY PIN
WAS INVENTED IN
1849 BY WALTER HUNT
IN 3 HOURS TO PAY OFF A
DEBT OF $15...HE SOLD
HIS MODEL AND IDEA FOR $400

A MATCH WHICH WILL
LIGHT 600 TIMES!
HAS BEEN INVENTED BY
DR. RINGER of Vienna.

DRAWN IN WIEN
May, 1931

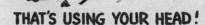

THAT'S USING YOUR HEAD!

JOHANN SCHMITT-BLANK (1824-1880)
PROFESSOR OF CLASSICAL LANGUAGES AT
THE UNIVERSITY OF FREIBURG, GERMANY,
KEPT HIMSELF COOL ON HOT DAYS
*BY WEARING A HIGH HAT
WITH A LID THAT COULD BE
RAISED OR LOWERED BY A
WIRE THAT EXTENDED
TO HIS POCKET*

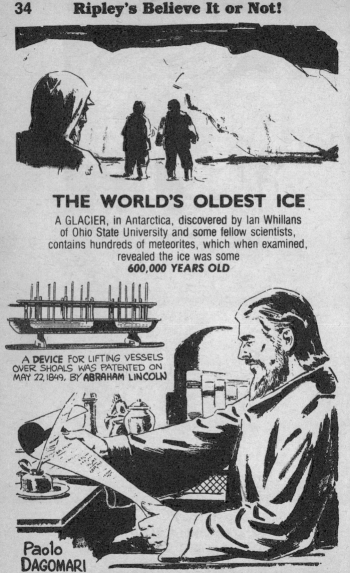

THE WORLD'S OLDEST ICE

A GLACIER, in Antarctica, discovered by Ian Whillans of Ohio State University and some fellow scientists, contains hundreds of meteorites, which when examined, revealed the ice was some
600,000 YEARS OLD

A **DEVICE** FOR LIFTING VESSELS OVER SHOALS WAS PATENTED ON MAY 22, 1849, BY **ABRAHAM LINCOLN**

Paolo **DAGOMARI** (1281-1372) AN ITALIAN MATHEMATICIAN, CONCEIVED THE USE OF THE COMMA *TO SEPARATE LARGE FIGURES INTO UNITS OF THREE*

SAMUEL F.B. MORSE
(1791-1872) WAS INSPIRED TO
INVENT THE MORSE CODE AND
THE TELEGRAPH BECAUSE NEWS
OF HIS WIFE'S DEATH CAME
TO HIM BY MAIL — —
SEVEN DAYS LATE

JOBST BÜRGI (1552-1631) of St. Gall, Switzerland CONCEIVED THE **SMALLEST INVENTION** IN HISTORY— *THE DECIMAL POINT!*

THOMAS A. EDISON (1847-1931) AMERICA'S MOST PROLIFIC INVENTOR, WAS GRANTED 1,093 PATENTS BY THE U.S. PATENT OFFICE, MORE THAN ANYONE ELSE-- YET THEY INCLUDED *SUCH DUDS AS A PERPETUAL CIGAR, FURNITURE MADE OF CEMENT AND A WAY OF USING GOLDENROD FOR RUBBER*

FLOKI RAFNA a Swedish Viking
DISCOVERED ICELAND IN 865
USING AS HIS ONLY NAVIGATION GUIDE
3 RAVENS
HE HAD NOTICED THAT RAVENS ALWAYS
CAME TO SWEDEN FROM THE NORTH
--SO HE RELEASED ONE OF HIS 3 BIRDS
EACH TIME HE NEEDED A BEARING

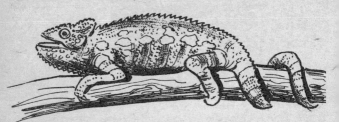

EUROPE AND AMERICA MOVING FARTHER APART

NASA SCIENTISTS, USING NEW AND PRECISE TECHNIQUES OF MEASURING, HAVE DETERMINED THAT THE NORTH AMERICAN AND EUROPEAN CONTINENTS ARE MOVING APART BY .59 INCHES EVERY YEAR

THE CHAMELEON

ACCORDING TO RECENT SCIENTIFIC STUDIES, DOES NOT CHANGE COLOR TO CAMOUFLAGE ITSELF BUT IN RESPONSE TO LIGHT AND TEMPERATURE CHANGES-- *AND TO EXPRESS ITS EMOTIONS*

HENRY HUDSON

SO IRKED ENGLAND BY DIS-
COVERING THE HUDSON RIVER
WHILE SAILING UNDER THE
DUTCH FLAG, THAT **HIS SHIP,
THE HALF MOON,** WAS SEIZED
AT DARTMOUTH, ENGLAND

A CLOCK
THAT GAVE YOU THREE GUESSES

A ONE-HAND CLOCK INVENTED BY BENJAMIN FRANKLIN IN 1770, *WAS NOT MARKETED UNTIL 200 YEARS LATER.*" THE HAND HERE READS EITHER 3:35, 7:35 OR 11:35, BUT FRANKLIN FIGURED ANYONE *WOULD KNOW ABOUT WHAT HOUR OF THE DAY IT WAS*

A **NEW SCALE**

THAT HAS A "VOICE," A "MEMORY" AND A VOCABULARY OF OVER 230 WORDS, MOTIVATES WEIGHT LOSS BY ALTERNATELY PRAISING OR SCOLDING UNTIL YOUR GOAL IS REACHED

TAKE IT OFF!

A TELEPHONE BOOTH

in Mansfield, Ohio,
is solar powered!.

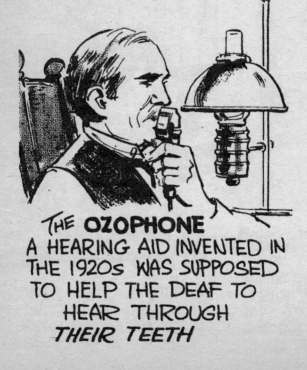

THE SECRET OF MAKING SILK WAS KNOWN ONLY TO THE CHINESE FOR 3,000 YEARS AND ANYONE WHO DISCLOSED IT TO FOREIGNERS WAS *PUT TO DEATH!*

THE **OZOPHONE** A HEARING AID INVENTED IN THE 1920s WAS SUPPOSED TO HELP THE DEAF TO HEAR THROUGH *THEIR TEETH*

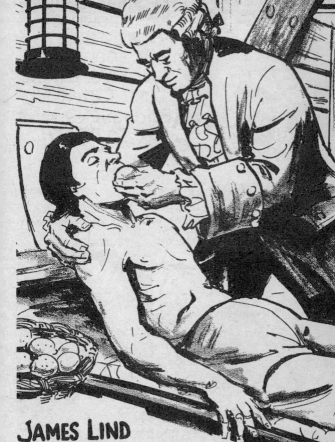

JAMES LIND
(1716-1794)
BY DISCOVERING THAT
CITRUS FRUITS OR JUICES COULD STAMP
OUT SCURVY, ELIMINATED THE DISEASE
*THAT KILLED MORE BRITISH SAILORS
IN WARTIME THAN DIED IN COMBAT*

DRUZHNAYA I
AN UNOCCUPIED SOVIET RESEARCH STATION IN THE
ANTARCTIC THAT DISAPPEARED IN OCT. 1986, WAS FOUND
FLOATING IN THE WEDDELL SEA ON A HUGE BLOCK
OF ICE 60 MILES BY 120 MILES (FEB. 1987)

"TETRA CITY"
A FLOATING ENTITY 9,000 FT. HIGH, PROPOSED BY
AMERICAN DESIGNER BUCKMINSTER FULLER TO RELIEVE
POPULATION DENSITY, WOULD FLOAT ON CONCRETE
PONTOONS IN ANY LARGE BODY OF WATER,
HOUSING SOME 1,000,000 PEOPLE

A REAL FLYING SAUCER

THE 200X, A SAUCER-SHAPED AIR-
CRAFT IN THE TESTING STAGE, HAS
EIGHT PROPELLERS, EACH DRIVEN
BY ITS OWN ENGINE, WHICH IS IN
ITS OWN TUNNEL IN THE CRAFT'S
BODY. INVENTED BY PAUL MOLLER
OF CALIFORNIA, WHO WANTS TO
PUT ONE IN EVERY GARAGE, IT
HAS MADE SEVERAL PEOPLE
THINK THEY'VE SEEN A UFO

JACK BROUGHTON
WHO BECAME THE BOXING
CHAMPION OF ENGLAND
IN 1734, CREATED AND
PUBLISHED THE FIRST
RULES FOR BOXERS
*AND INVENTED
THE MODERN
BOXING
GLOVE*

PEA KNIFE

Invented by HERBERT GREENE, Phila., Pa.

TO PREVENT PEAS FROM ROLLING OFF THE KNIFE
WHILE EATING!

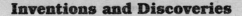

THERE
ARE MORE
STREETS
NAMED FOR
THIS
MAN
THAN ANY
OTHER MAN
IN THE WORLD

JOHN McADAM of Scotland
— THE COLOSSUS of ROADS

INVENTOR of THE MODERN PROCESS of PAVING
STREETS AND HIGHWAYS KNOWN AS
MACADAM

A **BENT RIFLE**
INVENTED IN 1894
WAS DESIGNED FOR USERS
*WHO WERE RIGHT-HANDED,
BUT LEFT-EYED*

**SIR KENELM
DIGBY** (1603-1665)
BRITISH NAVAL COMMANDER
INVENTED A SALVE SUPPOSED TO
BE ABLE TO HEAL A WOUND BY
BEING APPLIED *TO THE WEAPON
WHICH CAUSED IT*

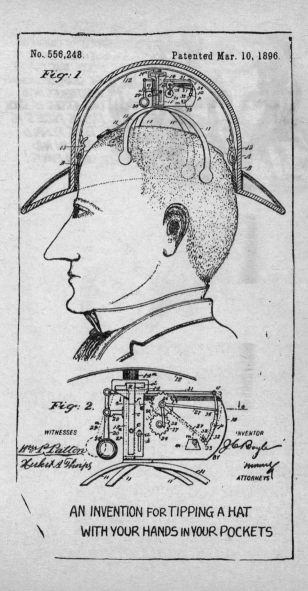

No. 556,248. Patented Mar. 10, 1896.

Fig: 1

Fig: 2

WITNESSES

INVENTOR

ATTORNEYS

AN INVENTION FOR TIPPING A HAT
WITH YOUR HANDS IN YOUR POCKETS

VEGIFORMS!
RICK TWEDDELL, OF CINCINNATI, OH, HAS INVENTED PLASTIC MOLDS THAT CHANGE THE SHAPE OF GROWING VEGETABLES INTO LIKENESSES OF SUCH FAMOUS PEOPLE AS ELVIS, RONALD REAGAN AND LINDA EVANS!

A **MOTH** (XANTHOPAN "PRAEDICTA") HAD ITS EXISTENCE PREDICTED BY ALFRED RUSSEL WALLACE BEFORE ANY SPECIMEN HAD BEEN FOUND BECAUSE THE NECTAR IN A TYPE OF MADAGASCAR ORCHID WAS REACHABLE ONLY BY A MOTH *WITH A 10-INCH PROBOSCIS*

BACTERIA
10,000 YEARS OLD, FOUND IN ICE AT McMURDO STATION IN THE ANTARCTIC IN 1974, *REVIVED ... AND REPRODUCED*

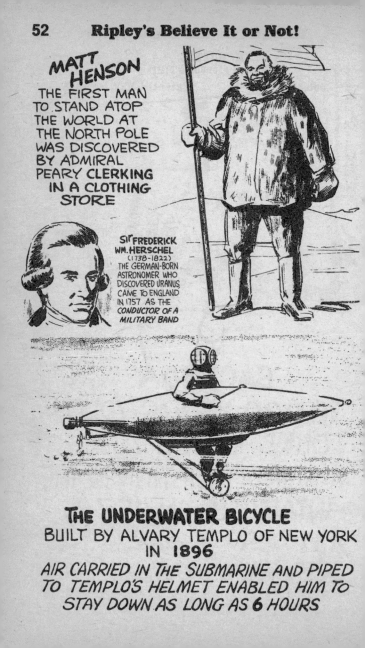

MATT HENSON
THE FIRST MAN TO STAND ATOP THE WORLD AT THE NORTH POLE WAS DISCOVERED BY ADMIRAL PEARY CLERKING IN A CLOTHING STORE

Sir FREDERICK WM. HERSCHEL (1738-1822) THE GERMAN-BORN ASTRONOMER WHO DISCOVERED URANUS CAME TO ENGLAND IN 1757 AS THE CONDUCTOR OF A MILITARY BAND

THE UNDERWATER BICYCLE
BUILT BY ALVARY TEMPLO OF NEW YORK IN **1896**
AIR CARRIED IN THE SUBMARINE AND PIPED TO TEMPLO'S HELMET ENABLED HIM TO STAY DOWN AS LONG AS 6 HOURS

M. GOETZE.
DEVICE FOR PRODUCING DIMPLES.

No. 560,351. Patented May 19, 1896

INVENTION
FOR MAKING
DIMPLES

Inventor
Martin Goetze

Geo H. Holgate
Attorney

Witnesses.
E. C. Wurdeman
J. J. Williamson

IN 1926 ROBERT H. GODDARD OF WORCHESTER, MA, THE FATHER OF ROCKET TECHNOLOGY, BUILT AND LAUNCHED A WORKING ROCKET WHICH ROSE 41 FEET INTO THE AIR AND LANDED 184 FEET FROM ITS LAUNCH PAD!

THE **OCTOBASSE** A MUSICAL INSTRUMENT INVENTED IN THE 19th CENTURY RESEMBLES A VIOLIN IN LOOKS BUT IS *10 FEET HIGH*

KING **HENRY III** (1551-1589) of France INVENTED THE FORK BECAUSE HE ALWAYS STAINED HIS LACE COLLAR EATING MEAT WITH HIS FINGERS

THE FIRST "AUTOMOBILE"

A MECHANICAL CARRIAGE,
THE PROPULSION POWER FOR
WHICH WAS NEVER REVEALED,
WAS DRIVEN THROUGH THE CITY
GATE OF MEMMINGEN, GERMANY,
IN 1447

TAWARIK MAKUTIN
ARAB MATHEMATICIAN
BLIND FROM **BIRTH**

INVENTED THE GREATEST OF
ALL MATHEMATICAL SYMBOLS

"O"

THE ZERO

HE CALLED IT—
*"THE NOTHINGNESS THAT I SEE,
ENCIRCLED BY A LINE"*

SKULLS
FROM BEFORE
THE IRON AGE
SHOW TOOTH
DECAY IN ONLY
2 TO 4 PERCENT
OF THOSE
EXAMINED
COMPARED TO
TODAY'S RATE
OF 40 TO 70
PERCENT

SIR HENRY **BESSEMER**

WHOSE PROCESS OF MAKING STEEL REVOLUTIONIZED
THE COMMERCIAL HISTORY OF THE WORLD
ALSO INVENTED THE POSTAGE STAMP
THE MOST WIDELY USED COMMODITY IN THE WORLD

THE HUMAN TARGET

ELLIOT WISBROD HAS BEEN SHOT AT MORE THAN ANY OTHER MAN IN THE WORLD
INVENTOR OF THE *BULLET-PROOF VEST*
—Chicago

SCIENTISTS IN BRITAIN HAVE DEVELOPED A TINY SEWING MACHINE THAT IS SWALLOWED BY A PATIENT THEN MANIPULATED FROM OUTSIDE THE BODY TO STITCH TISSUES TOGETHER!

ELISHA GRAVES OTIS (1811-1861) INVENTED HIS ELEVATOR WITHOUT EVER WORKING OUT THE DESIGN ON PAPER

PRETZELS
WERE INVENTED
IN SOUTHERN
FRANCE IN 610 A·D.
BY MONKS WHO
SHAPED THEM
TO LOOK LIKE
A CHILD'S ARMS
FOLDED IN
PRAYER

AN AMPHIBIOUS AUTOMOBILE
OF 1916, HAD A RUDDER AND PROPELLER SO IT COULD *BE DRIVEN ON LAND OR WATER*

PATENT #586,025
A DEVICE THAT SERVES AS A
COMBINATION *GRATER-SLICER*
AND *MOUSE AND FLY TRAP*
WAS REGISTERED AT THE
U.S. PATENT OFFICE
IN 1897!

THE SANDWICH WAS NAMED AFTER
THE EARL OF SANDWICH WHO INVENTED IT
IN ORDER TO HAVE A MEAL WITHOUT INTERRUPTING HIS CARD GAME
THE EARL WAS ALSO A FOP AND A POSEUR — IN OTHER WORDS A "HAM"

SIX-YEAR-OLD
COLLIN HAZEN
OF FARGO, N D,
HAS DESIGNED A
*BATTERY-POWERED
DOG COLLAR* THAT
GLOWS IN THE DARK!

A "PILL SWALLOWER" INVENTED IN THE 19th CENTURY HELPED DOCTORS GET MEDICATION INTO FEARFUL YOUNGSTERS

JOSEPH PRIESTLEY (1733-1804)
THE ENGLISH CHEMIST, CREATED SODA
WATER AFTER HE BECAME INTERESTED
IN THE FORMATION OF GASES
DURING FERMENTATION WHEN HE
MOVED NEXT DOOR TO A BREWERY

GEORGE CRUM

THE INDIAN CHEF AT A SARATOGA SPRINGS, N.Y., RESORT, INVENTED THE POTATO CHIP IN A FIT OF PIQUE ... WHEN A CUSTOMER COMPLAINED HIS FRENCH FRIES WERE TOO THICK, CRUM SHAVED THEM PAPER THIN -- *AND WAS ASTONISHED WHEN THEY BECAME POPULAR.*

LARGE-BRIMMED STRAW HATS
WERE WORN BY ITALIAN WOMEN IN THE 1400s, AND WHEN THEY WASHED THEIR HAIR IT WAS SPREAD OUT OVER THE BRIM TO DRY IN THE SUN

THE **FIRST FERRIS WHEEL**
DESIGNED BY GEORGE
FERRIS, WAS OPERATED
AT THE WORLD'S COLUMBIAN
EXPOSITION HELD IN
CHICAGO, ILL., IN 1893

THE **PYRAMID OF MEROË** in Egypt
CONTAINING THE TOMB OF QUEEN AMANI, WAS DEMOLISHED LAYER
BY LAYER BY DR. GIUSEPPE FERLINI, AN ITALIAN PHYSICIAN, IN 1834,
*BECAUSE IN A CHILDHOOD DREAM HE HAD SEEN THE PYRAMID AS
THE HIDING PLACE OF A GREAT TREASURE*-- FERLINI ACTUALLY FOUND
A TREASURE TROVE IN THE PYRAMID AND BECAME ENORMOUSLY WEALTHY

"TOM THUMB"
THE STEAM LOCOMOTIVE INVENTED BY PETER COOPER IN BALTIMORE, MD.,
RACED A HORSE-DRAWN CARRIAGE ON SEPT. 18, 1830 -- *AND LOST !*

THE FIRST U.S. PATENT

issued in 1790 and authorized by
President George Washington,
protected a new method for
MAKING SOAP.

GREGOR JOHANN MENDEL

(1822-1884) THE AUSTRIAN BOTANIST WHO DISCOVERED THE BASIC LAWS OF HEREDITY, NEVER WAS ABLE TO PASS THE EXAMINATION TO BECOME A FULL-FLEDGED TEACHER OF SCIENCE

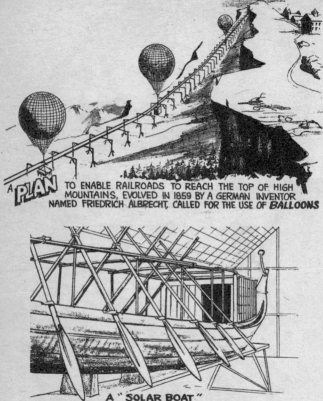

A **PLAN** TO ENABLE RAILROADS TO REACH THE TOP OF HIGH MOUNTAINS, EVOLVED IN 1859 BY A GERMAN INVENTOR NAMED FRIEDRICH ALBRECHT, CALLED FOR THE USE OF *BALLOONS*

A " SOLAR BOAT "
DISCOVERED IN EGYPT IN 1954 AND DESIGNED TO TRANSPORT THE PHARAOH CHEOPS TO HEAVEN, WAS IN EXCELLENT CONDITION— *DESPITE BEING SEALED IN HIS CRYPT FOR 4,600 YEARS!*

THE ZIPPER
WAS FIRST PATENTED IN 1851 BY ELIAS HOWE, INVENTOR OF THE SEWING MACHINE, BUT HE NEVER MARKETED THE ZIPPER AND CREDIT FOR ITS DISCOVERY USUALLY GOES TO WHITCOMB JUDSON, WHO PATENTED TWO SLIDE FASTENERS IN 1893 -- *42 YEARS AFTER HOWE*

A **HELMET GUN** INVENTED BY ALBERT PRATT OF VERMONT IN 1916, WAS FIRED WHEN THE WEARER *BLEW INTO A MOUTHPIECE*

"MOKELE-MBEMBE"

A DINOSAUR-LIKE BEAST, HAS BEEN SIGHTED SEVERAL TIMES IN THE AFRICAN CONGO'S LAKE TELLE AREA BY MANY PEOPLE, INCLUDING MEMBERS OF A SCIENTIFIC EXPEDITION -- ACCORDING TO THE SCIENTISTS IT COULD BE THE WORLD'S LAST SURVIVING DINOSAUR!

EIGHT-YEAR-OLD BRIAN BERLINSKI OF CLIFTON, N.J. INVENTED A SILENT CAR HORN FOR HEARING IMPAIRED DRIVERS! A LIGHT ON THE DASHBOARD FLASHES AT THE SOUND OF A HONKING HORN!

CHRISTOPHER LATHAM SHOLES
(1819-1890)

who perfected the typewriter,
started at age 48 and labored
on the project for the rest of his life— yet earned
only about $20,000 for his invention

SIR JOHN FLOYER
(1649-1734)
an English physician

INVENTED THE SECOND HAND
ON TIMEPIECES
*TO COUNT PATIENTS'
PULSE RATES!*

A PATENT FOR A DEVICE THAT WORKS AS A *COMBINED PLOW AND GUN* WAS FILED AT THE U.S. PATENT OFFICE IN 1862!

MICROSCOPIC FOSSILS

found in upstate New York in 1983, including an insect, a mite, a centipede and arachnids, are 380,000,000 years old — the oldest animals ever discovered in North America that were fully adapted to life on land!

THE DODO

WHICH EXISTED ONLY ON THE MASCARENE ISLANDS IN THE INDIAN OCEAN, WAS FIRST DISCOVERED IN 1598 AND BECAUSE IT WAS BOTH FEARLESS AND DEFENSELESS WAS EXTINCT *IN LESS THAN A CENTURY*

Francisco José de Caldas
naturalist and hero
of Colombia's independence

WHOSE NAME "CALDAS" MEANS "HOT WATER"

**INVENTED THE SYSTEM BY WHICH THE
HEIGHT OF A MOUNTAIN CAN BE
DETERMINED BY HOT WATER!**

*THERE IS A DEFINITE RATIO BETWEEN ALTITUDE
AND THE BOILING POINT OF WATER*

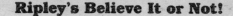
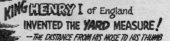

KING HENRY I of England INVENTED THE **YARD** MEASURE! —THE DISTANCE FROM HIS NOSE TO HIS THUMB

A **LIGHT CARRIAGE** PULLED BY KITES, WAS DESIGNED IN 1826 BY GEORGE POCOCK AND THE FOLLOWING YEAR IT DEFEATED IN A RACE THE DUKE OF GLOUCESTER'S CARRIAGE WHICH *WAS PULLED BY 4 HORSES*

A **SEWING MACHINE** POWERED BY THE HUMAN VOICE WAS INVENTED BY THOMAS EDISON WHO FELT THAT WOMEN WOULD *RATHER TALK THAN TREADLE*

JOHANN FRIEDRICH von STRUENSEE
(1731-1772)
WAS EXECUTED IN DENMARK
FOR CRIMES AGAINST THE STATE
-ONE OF THOSE CRIMES BEING
THE FACT THAT HE INVENTED
THE GAME CALLED BINGO

SUPER-PAPER

INVENTED BY DEREK BEST OF DAYTONA BEACH, FL., RESEMBLES PLAIN WHITE PAPER, BUT A SPECIAL PROCESS ENABLES THE SENDER TO PRINT ON IT SUGGESTIONS NOT VISIBLE TO THE NAKED EYE THAT CAN INFLUENCE THE RECIPIENT'S SUBCONSCIOUS MIND

A **DOGMOBILE** PATENTED IN THE U·S· IN 1870, PROVIDED FRONT-WHEEL DRIVE BY MEANS OF **2 DOGS** *RUNNING INSIDE A CAGE IN THE FRONT WHEEL*

SUITED TO YOUR MOOD

A NEW BATHING SUIT INVENTED BY DONALD SPECTOR OF UNION CITY, N.J., MADE OF MATERIAL THAT IS THERMALLY SENSITIVE, CHANGES COLOR AS ITS WEARER'S BODY TEMPERATURE FLUCTUATES INDICATING DIFFERENT MOODS

MR. and MRS. MICHAEL WRINTMORE
of Birdbrook, Halstead, Essex, England,
BOUGHT THEIR THATCHED-ROOF
COTTAGE IN FEBRUARY 1977,
FOR $18,000.
DIGGING UP ITS STONE FLOORS
5 MONTHS LATER THEY FOUND
99 ANCIENT GOLD SOVEREIGNS
VALUED AT $40,000

NATHANIEL BROWN PALMER (1799-1877)
AS CAPTAIN OF A U.S. SEALING SHIP IN 1820 DISCOVERED
THE CONTINENT OF ANTARCTICA AT THE AGE OF **21**

AN **INVENTION**
ACCORDING TO A DECISION
OF THE U.S. COURT
OF CUSTOMS AND PATENT
APPEALS, IS "SOMETIMES
...SIMPLY THE PRODUCT
OF *SHEER STUPIDITY*"

BOTTOMS UP!

TO HELP BEGINNERS,
THE LAID-BACK SKIERS'
ASSOC. HAS DEVELOPED
SPECIAL POSTERIOR
REGION SKIS FOR THOSE
WHO SPEND A LOT OF TIME
ON THEIR DERRIÉRES

PATENT #
3,552,388,
AN ELECTRICAL
DEVICE
DESIGNED TO
PUT A BABY TO
SLEEP *WITH A
SERIES OF
REGULAR PATS
ON THE BOTTOM,*
WAS FILED AT
THE U.S.
PATENT OFFICE!

BIRD-POWERED BALLOON

A BALLOON PATENTED IN THE U·S· IN 1887 BY
CHARLES R·E·WULFF OF PARIS, FRANCE,
WAS TO BE PROPELLED BY "LIVING MOTORS,"
CAPTIVE EAGLES, VULTURES AND CONDORS

SUITS AND DRESSES
TREATED WITH TWO CHEMICAL COMPOUNDS
CALLED PLASTIC CRYSTALS THAT HOLD
AND RELEASE HEAT, MAY BE ABLE TO
BE WORN ALL YEAR ROUND -- HEATING
UP IN WINTER AND COOLING
OFF IN SUMMER

A **PRICELESS PAINTING**
MADE OF HIS WIFE IN 1439,
BY FLEMISH ARTIST
JAN VAN EYCK,
WAS DISCOVERED IN 1808,
IN A FISH MARKET IN
BRUGES, BELGIUM, BEING
USED AS A TRAY ON WHICH
TO DISPLAY FISH

RENÉ ANTOINE de RÉAUMUR
THE FRENCH SCIENTIST,
DISCOVERED HOW TO MAKE
PAPER FROM WOOD BY
WATCHING WASPS MAKE
PAPERLIKE NESTS BY
CHEWING UP FOOD

A **FROZEN TUNNEL**
UNDER THE ENGLISH CHANNEL
WAS PROPOSED BY FRENCHMAN
AIMÉ THOMÉ DE GAMOND IN
THE 1800s. REFRIGERATION
COULD BE TURNED OFF TO
QUELL BRITISH FEARS OF
A FRENCH ATTACK

ELI WHITNEY

INVENTED THE COTTON GIN BEFORE HE HAD
EVER SEEN COTTON OR A COTTON SEED
*ALTHOUGH HIS INVENTION REVOLUTIONIZED THE INDUSTRY—
HE LOST MONEY ON IT*

FLYING AUTOMOBILE
WAS SUCCESSFULLY
FLOWN IN THE U.S. IN 1947
--BUT CRASHED BECAUSE THE
PILOT HAD FORGOTTEN TO
FILL ITS GAS TANK

THE TOOTHBRUSH
WAS INVENTED BY WILLIAM ADDIS
OF ENGLAND IN THE 1770s, WHILE
HE WAS INCARCERATED IN NEW-
GATE PRISON...HE BORED HOLES
IN A SMALL BONE, TIED STIFF
BRISTLES INTO TUFTS AND
INSERTED THEM IN THE HOLES

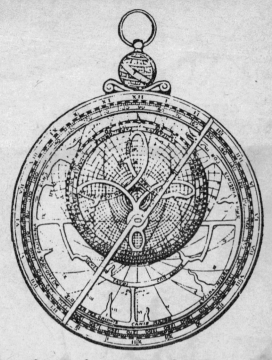

THE ASTROLABE
WHICH COULD DETERMINE
BOTH THE LATITUDE AND
TIME OF DAY, WAS
INVENTED IN GREECE
IN 150 B.C.-- THE
*WORLD'S OLDEST
SCIENTIFIC INSTRUMENT*

GETTING UP WITH A BANG
A 17th CENTURY PISTOL WITH A BUILT IN ALARM CLOCK!

EDGAR SIMS of Sun City, Ariz.
AT THE AGE OF 82 INVENTED A
DEVICE TO IMPROVE HEARING
-- MOUSE-LIKE EARS

THE OLDEST LIVING THING!

A RED CYPRESS STILL GROWING NEAR TAIPEI, TAIWAN, 173 FEET HIGH AND 88.44 FEET IN CIRCUMFERENCE, DISCOVERED BY PROF. CHOW HUI-YEN OF THE COLLEGE OF CHINESE CULTURE IN TAIWAN, IS MORE THAN 6,000 YEARS OLD

A **PRACTICAL HELICOPTER** WAS DESIGNED BY LEONARDO DA VINCI *MORE THAN 400 YEARS AGO*

The JIGSAW PUZZLE

was invented by English mapmaker John Spilsbury in **1760**

A PORTABLE DESK
INVENTED AND DESIGNED BY
THOMAS JEFFERSON WAS
THE ONE ON WHICH HE WROTE
*THE DECLARATION
OF INDEPENDENCE*

THE FIRST WHOLE DINOSAUR EGGS
EVER FOUND IN NO. AMERICA
WERE DISCOVERED
IN MONTANA ON
JULY 12, 1979

AN
EYEBALL MASSAGER
INVENTED IN 1931,
WAS OPERATED BY
*SQUEEZING ITS TWO
RUBBER CENTERS*

" THE **TURTLE** "

FIRST AMERICAN SUBMARINE
USED BY GEORGE WASHINGTON
IN THE REVOLUTIONARY WAR

Invented by
DAVID BUSHNELL

DINOSAURS
IN 140,000,000 YEARS ON EARTH,
RANGED FROM CHIPMUNK SIZE TO
HUGE BEASTS WEIGHING THOUSANDS
OF POUNDS--YET 40% OF ALL
KNOWN SPECIES HAVE BEEN
DISCOVERED ONLY SINCE THE
END OF THE 1960s

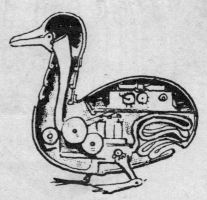

A MECHANICAL DUCK
INVENTED BY JACQUES
VAUCANSON OF FRANCE IN THE 1770s
FLUTTERED ITS WINGS, GROOMED
ITSELF, SWAM, PECKED AT FOOD—
AND ACTUALLY DIGESTED IT

GIGANTIC
MARBLE
STATUE
27½ FT. HIGH

TO BE
ERECTED
TO
**CAPTAIN
HANSON
GREGORY**
INVENTOR
OF THE
HOLE
IN THE
DOUGHNUT! Camden, Maine

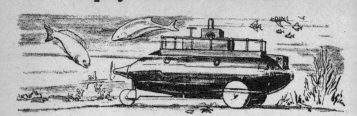

EVERY SUBMARINE
BUILT BY PIONEER
AMERICAN INVENTOR SIMON LAKE
WAS EQUIPPED WITH WHEELS
-SO IT COULD RIDE ALONG
THE BOTTOM OF THE SEA

Wilhelm
Konrad
ROENTGEN
(1845-1923)
THE GERMAN
PHYSICIST WHO
REVOLUTIONIZED
MEDICINE AND
SURGERY BY
DISCOVERING
THE X-RAY AND
WON THE FIRST
NOBEL PRIZE IN
PHYSICS, AS A
YOUTH WAS A
REBELLIOUS AND
UNINTERESTED
STUDENT

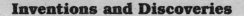

THE
FIRST MACHINE PISTOL
A REVOLVER INVENTED BY HENRY S. JOSSELYN OF ROXBURY, MASS., IN 1866, FIRED 20 BULLETS FROM A LONG CHAIN

A **STEAMSHIP**, 150 FEET LONG,
CONSTRUCTED BY JOUFFROY
D'ABBANS, MADE A SUCCESSFUL
CROSSING OF THE RIVER
SAONE, FROM LYON TO
ILE BARBE, A DISTANCE
OF FOUR MILES,
*20 YEARS BEFORE ROBERT
FULTON INVENTED HIS
STEAMBOAT* (July 15, 1783)

HALLEY'S COMET

ACCORDING TO
LATEST
SCIENTIFIC
RESEARCH,
WAS RELIABLY
RECORDED FOR
THE FIRST
TIME ON 2
BABYLONIAN
CLAY TABLETS
DATING BACK
TO **164** B.C.

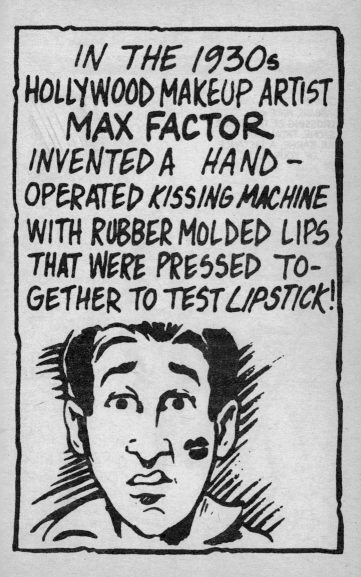

IN THE 1930s HOLLYWOOD MAKEUP ARTIST **MAX FACTOR** INVENTED A HAND-OPERATED *KISSING MACHINE* WITH RUBBER MOLDED LIPS THAT WERE PRESSED TO-GETHER TO TEST *LIPSTICK!*

DURING WORLD WAR II GEOFFREY PYKE OF ENGLAND WORKED AS A MILITARY ADVISOR AND MADE DESIGNS FOR AN UNSINKABLE BATTLE-SHIP MADE FROM A MIXTURE OF ICE AND WOOD PULP!

LOUIS BRAILLE THE FRENCHMAN WHO INVENTED A SYSTEM OF READING FOR THE BLIND, ADAPTED IT FROM MESSAGES USED BY FRENCH TROOPS WHO PUNCHED MARKS IN THICK PAPER SO THEY COULD BE READ AT NIGHT BY FEEL WITH-OUT USE OF A LIGHT

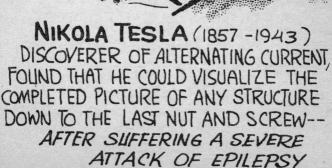

NIKOLA TESLA (1857 -1943)
DISCOVERER OF ALTERNATING CURRENT,
FOUND THAT HE COULD VISUALIZE THE
COMPLETED PICTURE OF ANY STRUCTURE
DOWN TO THE LAST NUT AND SCREW--
*AFTER SUFFERING A SEVERE
ATTACK OF EPILEPSY*

THE **BAGEL**
INVENTED IN 1683 BY A VIENNA COFFEE HOUSE OWNER WHO BAKED BREAD IN THE SHAPE OF THE CIRCULAR STIRRUPS OF KING JOHN III SOBIESKI OF POLAND--- TO HONOR HIM FOR OUSTING THE TURKS FROM VIENNA ··

A BIRD TRAP
IN WHICH A NET WAS SPRUNG WHEN FOOD WAS NIBBLED
-- INVENTED 3,000 YEARS AGO
FOUND IN A ROYAL TOMB IN THEBES, EGYPT

A CROSSWORD PUZZLE DICTIONARY

invented in the 1920s, was so small it could be strapped to the wrist

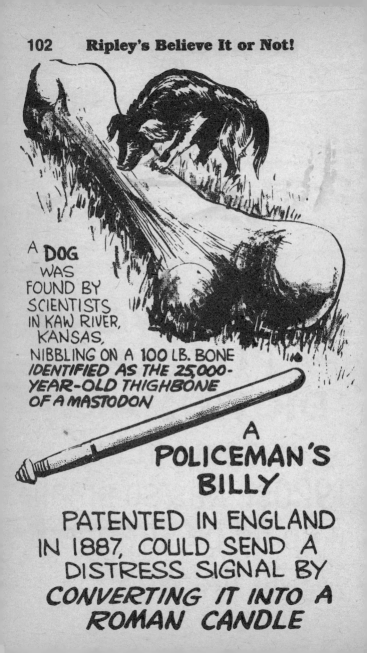

A **DOG** WAS FOUND BY SCIENTISTS IN KAW RIVER, KANSAS, NIBBLING ON A 100 LB. BONE *IDENTIFIED AS THE 25,000-YEAR-OLD THIGHBONE OF A MASTODON*

A **POLICEMAN'S BILLY**

PATENTED IN ENGLAND IN 1887, COULD SEND A DISTRESS SIGNAL BY *CONVERTING IT INTO A ROMAN CANDLE*

ABU'L HASSAN — Arabian Poet INVENTED THE HOUR - HE DIVIDED THE DAY AND NIGHT INTO 24 EQUAL PARTS IN THE 13TH CENTURY

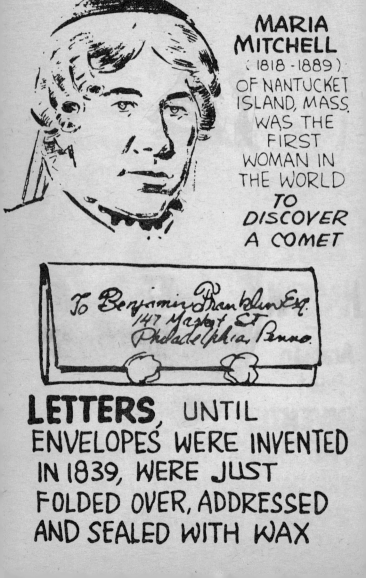

MARIA
MITCHELL
(1818 -1889)
OF NANTUCKET
ISLAND, MASS.
WAS THE
FIRST
WOMAN IN
THE WORLD
TO
DISCOVER
A COMET

To Benjamin Franklin Esq.
147 Market St
Philadelphia, Penna.

LETTERS, UNTIL
ENVELOPES WERE INVENTED
IN 1839, WERE JUST
FOLDED OVER, ADDRESSED
AND SEALED WITH WAX

THE REX

first discovered
in 1950 in England
is the only cat
with a natural
permanent — a coat
so tightly waved
it looks like part
OF ITS SKIN

A LIGHT BULB
3 FEET LONG,
MANUFACTURED IN JAPAN,
COULD OPERATE ON REGULAR
HOUSE CURRENT BUT WAS
47,300 TIMES BRIGHTER
THAN A NORMAL BULB !

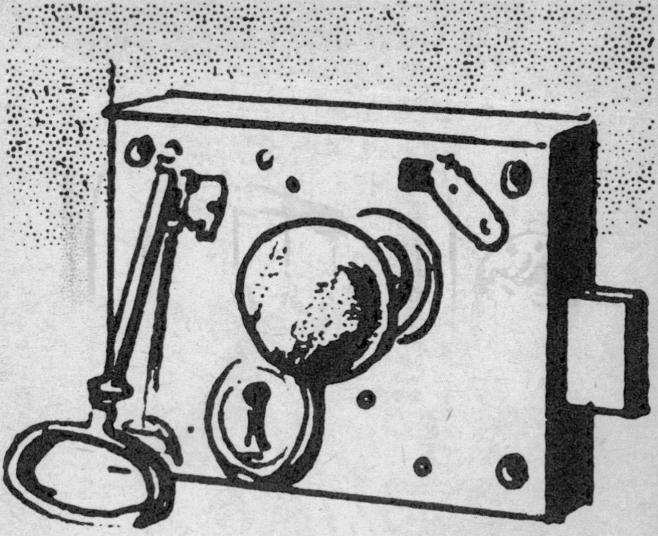

A **LOCK** INVENTED
IN THE 1800's,
HELD SMALL EXPLO-
SIVE CAPS AND
SURPRISED A BURGLAR
*BY EXPLODING WITH
A LOUD BANG*

THE FIRST PASSENGER ELEVATOR WAS DESIGNED FOR KING LOUIS XV OF FRANCE IN 1743! THE *FLYING CHAIR* RAN UP THE OUTSIDE OF THE PALACE AT VERSAILLES AND WAS *RAISED AND LOWERED BY HAND!*

A **SPANKING PADDLE** PATENTED IN THE U.S. IN 1953, HAD A JOINTED HANDLE DESIGNED *TO BREAK IF THE CHILD WAS SPANKED TOO FIRMLY*

A **CLAY TABLET**
FOUND IN IRAQ
AND MADE IN
2300 B.C., IS THE
OLDEST MAP IN
THE WORLD

IN 1876 ELISHA GRAY, OF OBERLIN, OH. APPLIED FOR A PATENT FOR THE TELEPHONE – *TWO HOURS AFTER ALEXANDER GRAHAM BELL PATENTED HIS INVENTION!*

THE FIRST BICYCLE
A STAINED GLASS WINDOW IN STOKE
POGES, ENGLAND, DEPICTING A
WINGLESS ANGEL ON A "BICYCLE,"
WAS CREATED IN THE 17th CENTURY
*--NEARLY 200 YEARS BEFORE
THE INVENTION OF THE BICYCLE*

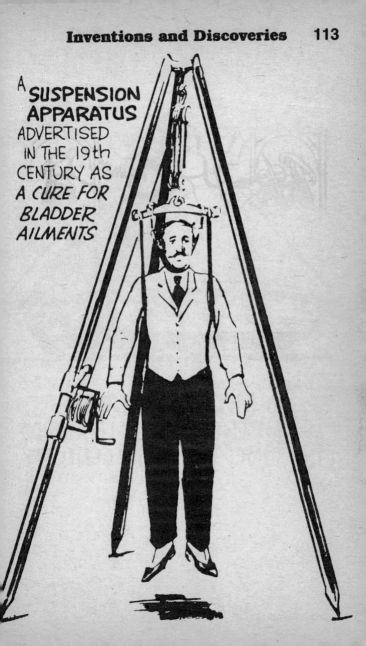

A **SUSPENSION APPARATUS** ADVERTISED IN THE 19th CENTURY AS A *CURE FOR BLADDER AILMENTS*

A MILITARY TANK
WAS DESIGNED BY LEONARDO DA VINCI IN THE 15th CENTURY

A **STEAM-POWERED AIRCRAFT**
BUILT IN 1894 BY SIR HIRAM
MAXIM, HAD 4,000 SQ. FEET OF WINGS
AND WEIGHED 8,000 POUNDS
IT NEVER GOT OFF THE GROUND

THE OLDEST PRINTED BOOK
A BOOK FOUND WALLED UP
IN A CAVE ON THE BORDER
OF TURKESTAN AND CHINA,
WAS PRINTED BY WANG CHIEH
1,105 YEARS AGO

THE FIRST ICE-MAKING MACHINE PATENTED IN 1851 BY DR. JOHN GORRIE OF APALACHICOLA, FLA., TO COOL HOSPITAL ROOMS, WAS A FINANCIAL FAILURE BECAUSE IT WAS DENOUNCED AS "TOO FANTASTIC"

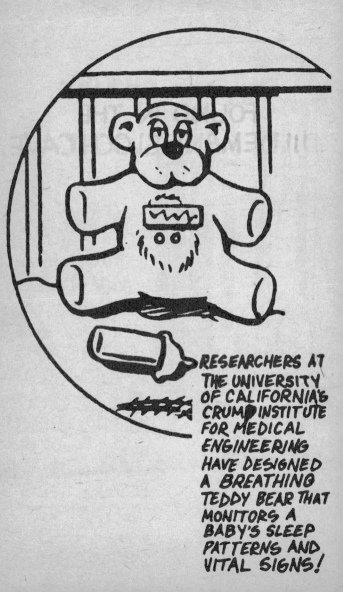

RESEARCHERS AT THE UNIVERSITY OF CALIFORNIA'S CRUMP INSTITUTE FOR MEDICAL ENGINEERING HAVE DESIGNED A *BREATHING* TEDDY BEAR THAT MONITORS A BABY'S SLEEP PATTERNS AND VITAL SIGNS!

THE OLDEST STATUE OF THE HUMAN FIGURE

FOUND IN THE WILDEMANLISLOCH CAVE, SWITZERLAND, --CREATED 70,000 YEARS AGO

TWO SCIENTISTS

Robert De Vries and Roy Tuft,
have patented a method of branding
diamonds by bombarding them with
electrically charged atoms, which
assures easy identification
yet leaves the stones unmarred

AN *ALARM CLOCK* created in England in 1600, AWAKENED ITS OWNER BY *FIRING A BLANK CARTRIDGE*

"THE JOGGER" A **ROCK DRAWING** OF A RUNNING MAN, FOUND AT Tassili -n-Ajjer, IN THE SAHARA DESERT, DATES BACK TO **8,000** B·C.

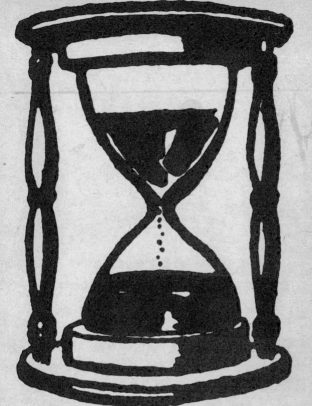

THE HOURGLASS
WAS INVENTED
FOR THE PURPOSE OF
LIMITING THE LENGTH
OF SERMONS

A LIVE CATFISH
WAS FOUND BY LUMBERMEN
in Tuscarawas Park, in New
Philadelphia, Ohio, IN A
WATER-FILLED DEPRESSION IN A TREE
40 FEET ABOVE THE GROUND—
THE FISH WAS DROPPED INTO
A LAKE AND SWAM AWAY

THE WHEEL HAS BEEN RE-INVENTED

SYDNEY JONES of Great Malvern, England, has invented a new wheel made of elastic spring steel that allows its rim to fold around obstacles and roll over them as if *ON A CUSHION OF AIR*